United States Olympic Committee

ICE HOCKEY

Mrs. Perry's Preschool

Griffin Publishing Group
Glendale, California

Ice hockey is a team sport.

It is played on an ice rink.

An ice hockey game has three periods.

There are two teams.
Each team has six players.

The players wear thick pads and a helmet for protection.

The players skate on the ice.

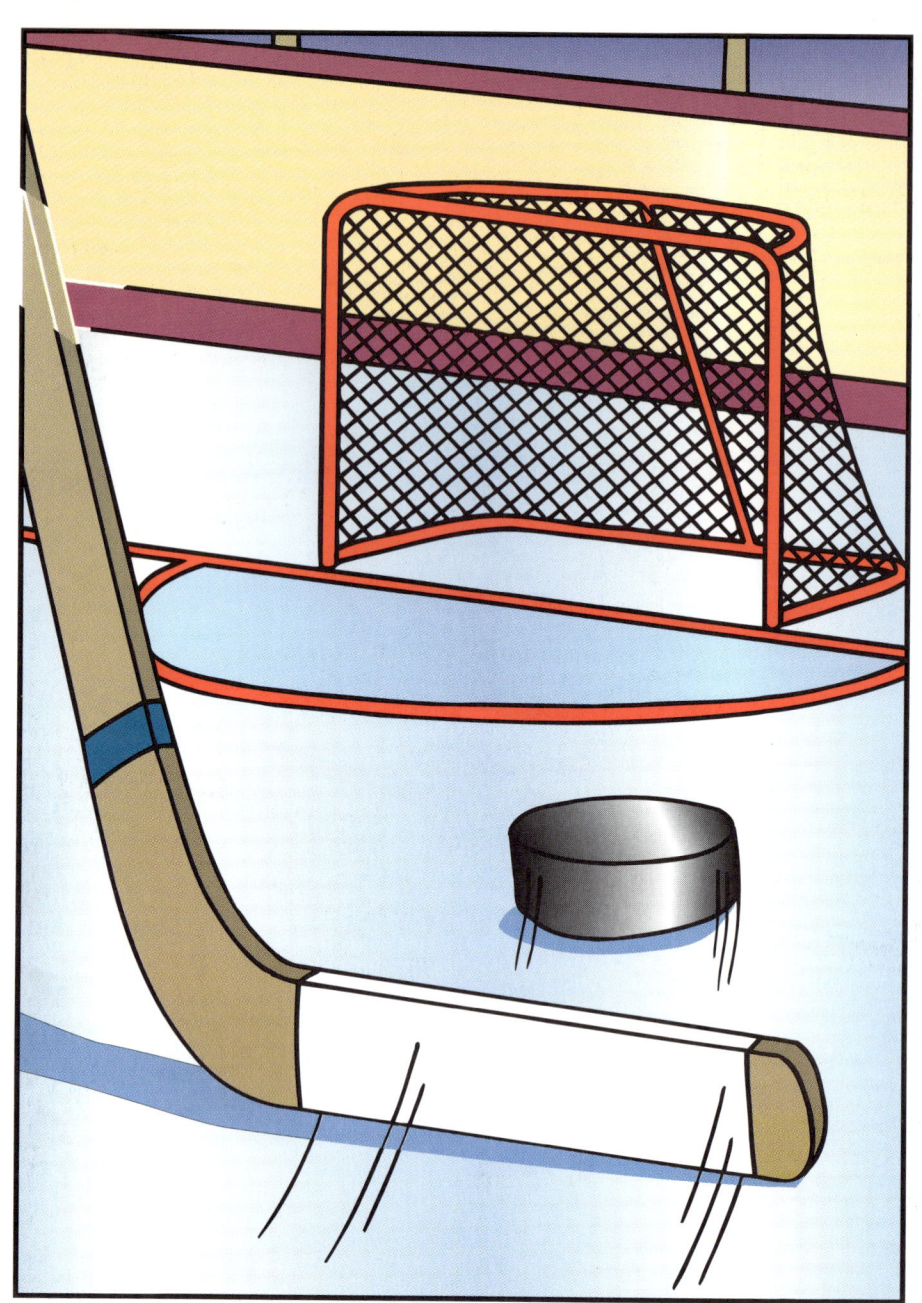

Each player has a stick. There are two nets and one puck.

Players use the stick to move the puck.

They pass the puck to a teammate.

They try to shoot the puck into the net.

They try to stop the other team from getting the puck.

Each team has a goaltender.

He tries to stop the puck.

A goal is scored when the puck goes into the net.

The players are happy when their team scores.